SCHOLASTIC

BANISH BORING WORDS!

Leilen Shelton

NEW YORK • TORONTO • LONDON • AUCKLAND • SYDNEY
MEXICO CITY • NEW DELHI • HONG KONG • BUENOS AIRES

Teaching *Resources*

To the teachers at Talbert, especially Amy Junge, Heather Harrison, and Donna Fraga, who generously shared their ideas; to Beth Fockler at Fulton for mentoring me early on; and to friend/fellow teacher Jennifer Mendoza.

To my principal, Cathie Abdel, who has always made me feel like a million bucks; to Fountain Valley School District Superintendent Rosemarie Eadie who has been an incredible source of encouragement over the years.

To my tutoring students Alexis Coco, Mark Gale, Mike Gale, Kate Gasparro, Matt Gasparro, Anthony Ho, Jacqueline Ho, Joshua Lim, Leslie Lim, Sarah Lo, Tiffany Lo, Jason Mar, Sean Myers, Ryan Nguyen, Jeffrey Wang, and Justine Wang.

Thank you, Donna, for cheering me on. Thank you Mom for watching the kids so many times while I worked on the book with Dad. Thank you, thank you, thank you, Dad. Without your countless hours invested in the typesetting, editing, and design of this book, it never would have happened. I owe you BIG TIME, Nudgy!

To Myles for knowing just when Mommy needed you to take a nap, to Sydney who brings so much love and joy to my life, and to my husband, Jason, who has always supported me. I'm blessed to have a partner like you.

Editor: Sarah Longhi
Cover design by Jason Robinson
Interior design by Gene Toth
ISBN-13: 978-0-545-08303-4
ISBN-10: 0-545-08303-6

12 13 14 15 16   40   16 15 14

Table of Contents

Introduction

During my first year as a middle school teacher, I quickly discovered that my students had wonderful ideas for their writing, but struggled to express them clearly and descriptively. They recognized strong and specific words, but couldn't always retrieve them on their own, and using a thesaurus was time-consuming. What they needed was a fast and easy way to find the "right" words for their writing.

I developed a list of action verbs, which led to a list of more specific movement words. Other word lists followed, and I soon had enough lists to make a small booklet for each student to use. I was thrilled with the remarkable improvements in their writing and in their confidence. They were so proud of their ability to choose their words so precisely and powerfully.

The booklet circulated to other teachers, and it wasn't long before almost every English teacher at my school was using the booklet. Within a year's time, the booklet began showing up with the students I privately tutored—students who attended *other* schools in my district. Apparently, I wasn't the only teacher searching for ways to empower students with strong, specific words. I'm excited to share the culmination of that effort with you in this book.

Banish Boring Words—a collection of word lists containing dozens of options for frequently used words and phrases—supports all types of writing. In some ways, it is like a condensed thesaurus. The purpose of this book is to provide students with shortcuts to finding descriptive words that will enable them to write with greater clarity and sophistication. It is my hope that this book helps students achieve their full potential as writers.

How to Use This Book

The word lists are arranged by topics so students can flip quickly between related pages, and example sentences are provided under the title of each word list to demonstrate how each page should be used.

Some suggestions for using this book flexibly in the classroom include:

- Making copies of the word lists for each student to use during independent writing time.
- Providing copies of the word lists for groups of students to use as a resource during writing workshop.
- Photocopying one word list or section at a time when introducing a new lesson. For example, you might use the Character Traits list (page 36) during a lesson on character development.
- Copying word lists for vocabulary-building exercises, including games and test preparation for English language learners.
- Making poster-size copies of the lists to serve as "word walls" in the classroom— visible and accessible resources for interesting words.

For more information, visit my Web site at **www.leilenshelton.com.**

Transitions

For the Beginning

A bad	At the beginning	Initially	One important
A good	Before	In the beginning	The first
An important	Early on	In the first place	To begin
As soon as	First	It started when	To start
At first	First of all	One	Yesterday

For the Middle

A better	Another important	Furthermore	Next
Accordingly	A second	However	Second
Additionally	At the same time	In addition	Secondly
After	A worse	In fact	Shortly thereafter
After that	Before long	In the meantime	Soon after
Afterward	Besides	Later	Suddenly
All at once	During	Later on	Then
All of a sudden	Equally important	Likewise	The next
Along with	Following this	Meanwhile	The second
Also	For example	More importantly	When
Another	For instance	Moreover	While

For the End

Accordingly	For this reason	Later on	Therefore
A final	Furthermore	Moreover	The worst
After	Hence	Most importantly	Thus
After that	In brief	Obviously	To conclude
All at once	In conclusion	Of course	To summarize
All in all	In fact	On the whole	To sum up
All of a sudden	In other words	Shortly thereafter	To this end
As a result	In short	Since	Ultimately
At last	In summary	Soon after	Undeniably
At the end	In the end	The best	Undoubtedly
Clearly	Last	The final	When
Consequently	Last of all	The last	With this in mind
Eventually	Lastly	The most important	Without a doubt
Finally	Later	Then	Without question

Essay Verbs for Writing About...

Z-Z-Z-Z-Z *Boring:* The article "Butterflies" <u>is about</u> the migration habits of butterflies.
Interesting: The article "Butterflies" <u>investigates</u> the migration habits of butterflies.

Characters

attempts	determines	experiences	learns	strives
battles	discovers	faces	realizes	struggles
competes	encounters	figures out	recognizes	undergoes
copes	endeavors	finds out	seeks	understands
deals with	endures	grapples with	sets out	undertakes

Compare/Contrast Texts

analyzes	contrasts	emphasizes	explores	identifies
classifies	considers	examines	focuses on	presents
compares	deals with	explains	highlights	points out

Descriptions

depicts	describes	illustrates	portrays	presents

Informational/Expository Texts

analyzes	defines	explores	identifies	provides
answers	describes	features	informs	reports
classifies	examines	focuses on	investigates	reveals
deals with	explains	highlights	presents	traces

Messages/Lessons

advises	expresses	illustrates	reminds	stresses
demonstrates	focuses on	implies	reveals	suggests
emphasizes	illuminates	points out	shows	teaches

Narrative Stories

chronicles	describes	follows	presents	retells
deals with	details	illustrates	recounts	tells about
depicts	explores	narrates	relates	traces

Persuasive Texts

addresses	contends	discourages	exposes	reasons
advises	convinces	disputes	focuses on	recommends
argues	criticizes	emphasizes	insists	refutes
asserts	deals with	encourages	points out	rejects
claims	defends	evaluates	praises	suggests
confronts	denies	examines	proposes	supports

Movements

Fast

biked	jerked	skittered
bolted	jolted	slammed
bounded	jostled	slapped
burst	jumped	slashed
bustled	kicked	sliced
charged	knocked	smacked
chased	lashed	smashed
clamored	leapt	snapped
crashed	lunged	snatched
darted	mauled	sped
dashed	nabbed	sprang
dodged	outpaced	sprinted
dove	outran	stampeded
erupted	plunged	streaked
flailed	pounced	swiped
fled	quickened	swooped
flew	raced	tackled
frisked	ran	tore
galloped	rode	trotted
grabbed	rushed	whirred
grasped	scampered	whisked
gunned	scooted	whizzed
hastened	scrambled	wrestled
hightailed	scurried	yanked
hurried	scuttled	zapped
hustled	shot	zigzagged
jabbed	shoved	zipped
jammed	skipped	zoomed

Slow

ambled	loitered	staggered
biked	lollygagged	stalked
brewed	lounged	stamped
coasted	lugged	stepped
crawled	lumbered	stomped
crept	lurked	straggled
cruised	marched	strayed
dawdled	meandered	strode
dillydallied	moped	stroked
dragged	moseyed	strolled
drifted	napped	strutted
dripped	paced	swaggered
edged	plodded	swayed
floated	plopped	tiptoed
flowed	poked	toddled
frolicked	prowled	trailed
froze	relaxed	traipsed
gallivanted	roamed	traversed
glided	rocked	treaded
hiked	roved	trekked
hobbled	sauntered	tromped
inched	shuffled	trooped
jogged	skipped	trudged
journeyed	slinked	undulate
lagged	slithered	ventured
limped	slogged	waited
lingered	slowed	walked
loafed	snuck	wallowed
lobbed	sputtered	wandered

Action Verbs

arrived
alighted
appeared
disembarked
dismounted
entered
landed
reached

ate
attacked
chowed
consumed
devoured
feasted
gobbled
gorged
grazed
inhaled
munched
nibbled
noshed
pecked
picked
porked
scarfed
snacked
wolfed

attacked
ambushed
assaulted
besieged
bombarded
charged
combated
infiltrated
invaded
jumped
mugged

overwhelmed
pounced
raided
rushed
stormed
struck

began
activated
commenced
incited
initiated
instigated
instituted
introduced
launched
originated
pioneered
started

broke
busted
cracked
crushed
demolished
fractured
severed
shattered
smashed
snapped
split
tore

bumped
banged
bounced
butted
collided
jarred
jerked

jolted
jostled
knocked
pounded
rattled
shook
slammed
smacked
thudded
thumped
thwacked

caught
apprehended
bagged
busted
captured
hooked
lassoed
nabbed
nailed
netted
plucked
snagged
snared
snatched

changed
adapted
altered
converted
evolved
metamorphosed
modified
mutated
reformed
remodeled
renovated
reorganized
restyled

revolutionized
transfigured
transformed
transposed

chased
charged
drove
followed
hounded
hunted
pursued
rushed
sped
tracked
trailed

cheered
applauded
clapped
hailed
praised
rooted
saluted
yelled

clapped
applauded
cheered
patted
slapped

climbed
ascended
clambered
crawled
escalated
mounted
rose
scaled
soared

Action Verbs

closed
blocked
bolted
buttoned
clenched
clogged
corked
locked
obstructed
plugged
screened
sealed
shut
stuffed

covered
blanketed
buried
camouflaged
carpeted
cloaked
clothed
coated
concealed
disguised
eclipsed
enclosed
enfolded
enshrouded
enveloped
hid
masked
obscured
screened
shaded
shrouded
veiled
wrapped

crashed
crunched
sideswiped
smashed
totaled

cried
bawled
bemoaned
bewailed
blubbered
grieved
groaned
howled
lamented
moaned
mourned
sniffed
sniveled
sobbed
wailed
wept
whimpered
whined

cut
amputated
carved
chiseled
chopped
cleaved
clipped
cropped
curtailed
diced
gashed
hacked
lacerated
lopped
nicked
pierced
punctured
ripped
sheared
slashed
sliced
slit
snipped
split
whacked

danced
boogied
frolicked
hopped
hustled
jigged
jitterbugged
jived
jumped
leapt
pranced
rocked
shimmied
spun
strutted
swayed
swung
tangoed
tapped
twisted
waltzed
whirled

destroyed
annihilated
crushed
decimated
demolished
eradicated
exterminated
extinguished
leveled
quashed
quelled
ravaged
razed
ruined
sabotaged
shattered
smashed
totaled
trashed
vandalized
wasted
wrecked

disappeared
absconded
dissolved
ebbed
evanesced
evaporated
faded
fled
melted
receded
retreated
vanished
waned

dragged
hauled
lugged
schlepped
towed
trailed
transported
tugged
yanked

drank
chugged
consumed
downed
gargled
gulped
guzzled
lapped
sipped
slurped
swallowed
swigged
toasted

escaped
absconded
bolted
circumvented
deserted
disappeared

escaped (cont'd)
dodged
ducked
eluded
evaded
fled

exploded
backfired
blasted
blazed
burst
detonated
erupted
ruptured
shattered
split
thundered

fell
collapsed
declined
descended
dropped
plunged
poured
stumbled
sunk
toppled
tottered
tripped
tumbled

fixed
adjusted
corrected
doctored
mended
overhauled
patched
rebuilt
reconstructed
repaired
restored
revamped

flew
buzzed
circled
crossed
darted
dashed
dove
drifted
floated
fluttered
glided
hovered
jetted
maneuvered
scudded
skimmed
soared
swooped
whisked
whooshed
zipped
zoomed

fought
battled
bickered
boxed
brawled
clashed
contended
disputed
dueled
feuded
grappled
jousted
quarreled
scuffled
skirmished
sparred
tussled
warred
wrestled

found
discovered
located
pinpointed
recovered
spotted
uncovered
unearthed

gathered
aggregated
assembled
clustered
collected
congregated
convened
converged
corralled
crowded
flocked
herded
hoarded
huddled
rallied
reunited
stockpiled
swarmed
thronged
united

gave
awarded
bequeathed
bestowed
conferred
contributed
donated
endowed
entrusted
gifted
granted
handed
presented
provided

relinquished
supplied

grew
abounded
amplified
broadened
developed
doubled
enlarged
expanded
extended
flourished
heightened
increased
inflated
lengthened
matured
multiplied
produced
rose
shot
spread
sprouted
stretched
swelled
thickened
waxed
widened

held
clasped
cleaved
clenched
clung
clutched
cradled
embraced
enclosed
grasped
gripped
hugged
palmed
squeezed

...more Action Verbs

hit
bashed
beat
boxed
clipped
clobbered
clocked
clubbed
cuffed
flailed
hooked
jabbed
knocked
nailed
pelted
popped
pounded
punched
slapped
slugged
smacked
socked
struck
swatted
thrashed
thumped
walloped
whacked

hugged
clung
cradled
cuddled
embraced
enfolded
enveloped
grasped
nestled
pressed
squeezed

hung
attached
dangled

draped
drooped
fastened
hooked
suspended

hurt
abused
ached
afflicted
ailed
belted
bit
bruised
burned
cut
disabled
flailed
flogged
harmed
impaired
injured
kicked
lacerated
lashed
mauled
nipped
pierced
pinched
pricked
pummeled
punched
punctured
slapped
slugged
squeezed
stabbed
stung
throbbed
tore
whacked
whipped
wounded
wrung

jumped
bobbed
bounced
bucked
cantered
dove
hopped
hurdled
jerked
leapt
loped
lunged
lurched
parachuted
plummeted
skipped
sprang
tripped
vaulted

laughed
burst
chortled
chuckled
giggled
guffawed
hee-hawed
howled
roared
screamed
shrieked
simpered
snickered
sniggered
snorted
tee-heed
tittered
whooped

left
abandoned
departed
deserted

disappeared
ditched
eloped
embarked
escaped
exited
fled
scrammed
split
vacated
vanished
withdrew

made
assembled
built
constructed
created
fashioned
forged
formed
framed
invented
manufactured
produced
shaped

mended
cured
doctored
fixed
healed
improved
patched
rebuilt
reconstructed
recovered
recuperated
remedied
repaired
restored
revised

...even more Action Verbs

opened
bore
burst
cleared
exposed
jimmied
revealed
ruptured
slit
spread
unblocked
unbolted
uncorked
uncovered
unfastened
unfurled
unlatched
unlocked
unsealed
unwrapped
vented
ventilated

planned
arranged
brainstormed
devised
engineered
formulated
mapped
organized
outlined
plotted
schemed
sketched
strategized

played
cavorted
clowned
frolicked
reveled
romped

pulled
dragged
hauled
heaved
jerked
lugged
plucked
schlepped
towed
tugged
wrenched
yanked

pushed
bulldozed
crowded
elbowed
gored
impelled
jammed
jostled
launched
muscled
nudged
poked
railroaded
rammed
shouldered
shoved
squashed
squeezed
squished
steamrolled
thrust

reached
extended
grasped
lunged
seized
strained
stretched

repaired
cured
doctored
fixed
healed
improved
mended
patched
rebuilt
reconstructed
recovered
recuperated
restored
revised

ripped
clawed
frayed
gashed
shredded
slashed
slit
split
tore

shook
chattered
jarred
jerked
jogged
joggled
jolted

quaked
quivered
rattled
reeled
rocked
ruffled
shimmered
shimmied
shivered
shuddered
swayed
tottered
trembled
tremored
twittered
vibrated
waggled
waved
wobbled

shrunk
compressed
condensed
constricted
contracted
decreased
deflated
diminished
dwindled
lessened
narrowed
reduced
shortened
shriveled
waned
wasted
weakened
withered
wrinkled

skipped
bounded
cantered
flitted
hippety-hopped
hopped
leapt
pranced
scampered
scooted
skedaddled
skittered
sprang

slept
catnapped
crashed
dozed
dreamed
hibernated
napped
reposed
retired
slumbered
snoozed
snored

smiled
beamed
grinned
simpered
smirked

spun
gyrated
pirouetted
reeled
revolved
rotated
twirled

...even more Action Verbs

spun (cont'd)
twisted
wheeled
whirled

stayed
continued
lodged
remained
sojourned
visited

stole
abducted
blackmailed
burglarized
cheated
defrauded
embezzled
filched
fleeced
kidnapped
lifted
looted
pilfered
pillaged
pinched
pirated
plagiarized
plundered
poached
purloined
ransacked
shoplifted
snatched
stripped
swindled
swiped
thieved

stopped
barred
blocked
ceased
discontinued
disrupted
finished
halted
hindered
impeded
intercepted
obstructed
paused
quit
refrained
restrained
stalled
terminated

suffered
ached
agonized
ailed
endured
grieved
strained
tormented
winced
writhed

surrounded
besieged
circled
encased
encircled
enclosed
encompassed
engulfed
inundated
wrapped

swam
bathed
dove
floated
glided
paddled
raced
stroked
submerged
waded

swung
dangled
flapped
oscillated
pivoted
rocked
swayed
swerved
swiveled
twirled
whirled

threw
catapulted
chucked
fired
flung
hurled
launched
lobbed
pegged
pelted
pitched
scattered
showered
tossed
volleyed

took
abducted
bagged
borrowed
captured
clutched
commandeered
confiscated
filched
grabbed
hooked
lifted
nabbed
pinched
plucked
pocketed
seized
snagged
snatched
stole
swiped

trapped
ambushed
beguiled
cornered
corralled
deceived
duped
ensnared
entangled
entrapped
fooled

tricked
bamboozled
beguiled
charmed

cheated
conned
confused
deceived
defrauded
duped
fooled
hoodwinked
misled
outwitted
scammed
shafted
swindled
trapped

twisted
coiled
contorted
corkscrewed
curled
entwined
intertwined
spiraled
spun
squirmed
swiveled
turned
twined
twirled
weaved
wiggled
wound
wrapped
wrenched
wriggled
writhed
wrung
zigzagged

"Said" Synonyms

Z-Z-Z-Z-z **Boring:** "I don't want to go," she <u>said</u>.
Interesting: "I don't want to go!" she <u>whimpered</u>.

agreed
acknowledged
assented
conceded
concurred
consented
seconded

animal sounds
barked
chirped
croaked
crowed
growled
hissed
howled
panted
roared
snarled
squawked
squeaked
yapped
yelped

answered
reacted
remarked
replied
responded
retorted
returned

argued
bickered
contended
contested
contradicted
countered
debated
denied
disagreed
disputed

objected
opposed
protested
quarreled
quibbled
squabbled

asked
challenged
grilled
inquired
interrogated
pried
probed
queried
questioned
quizzed
requested

begged
beseeched
entreated
implored
petitioned
pleaded
prayed
pressed
requested
urged

blamed
accused
alleged
attacked
charged
claimed
rebuked
reproved

chatted
babbled
blabbed

chitchatted
gabbed
gibbered
gossiped
jabbered
prattled

commented
mentioned
noted
opined
remarked
stated

complained
bemoaned
bewailed
fretted
fussed
griped
groaned
grumbled
moaned
pouted
sniveled
whimpered
whined
yammered

cried
bawled
bemoaned
bewailed
blubbered
grieved
groaned
howled
lamented
moaned
mourned

sighed
sniffled
sniveled
sobbed
wailed
wept
whimpered
yammered
yowled

criticized
blasted
chastised
chided
disapproved
lambasted
nitpicked
reprimanded
zinged

declared
announced
asserted
broadcasted
confirmed
informed
proclaimed
professed

exaggerated
boasted
bragged
distorted
elaborated
embellished
enhanced
expanded
expounded
fabricated
inflated

romanticized
overstated

explained
clarified
described
detailed
illustrated
interpreted
paraphrased
summarized
translated

gasped
choked
gulped
heaved
panted
snorted
wheezed

imitated
aped
echoed
impersonated
mimicked
mocked
parodied
parroted

interrupted
blurted
inserted
interfered
interjected

intimidated
badgered
browbeat
bullied
coerced
harassed
hounded

"Said" Synonyms

intimidated
(cont'd)
taunted
threatened

joked
bantered
jested
jived
joshed
kidded

laughed
cackled
chortled
chuckled
giggled
howled
roared
snickered
sniggered
snorted

nagged
badgered
hounded
needled
pestered
prodded

observed
detected
discerned
discovered
noted
noticed
perceived

ordered
charged
commanded
decreed
demanded
directed
instructed

persuaded
cajoled
coaxed
convinced
exhorted
insisted
urged
wheedled
wooed

predicted
conjectured
forecasted
foretold
guessed
inferred
presumed
prognosticated
prophesied
speculated
supposed
surmised

promised
agreed
assured
ensured
guaranteed
pledged
swore
vowed

raged
boiled
bristled
foamed
fumed
ranted
raved
spit
stormed

rejoiced
celebrated
cheered
exulted
hooted
jubilated
reveled

remembered
brooded
recalled
recollected
reflected
reminisced

retold
narrated
quoted
recited
recounted
repeated

revealed
announced
confessed
confided
declared
disclosed
divulged
expressed
proclaimed
professed
uttered

sang
chanted
chirped
crooned
hummed
serenaded
trilled

twittered
warbled
yodeled

scolded
berated
chastened
chided
criticized
lectured
rebuked
reprimanded
reproached

screamed
bawled
bellowed
blared
blurted
cried
exclaimed
hollered
roared
shouted
shrieked
shrilled
squealed
wailed
yelled
yowled

stuttered
faltered
hesitated
sputtered
stammered
stumbled
trembled

suggested
advised
hinted
implied

inferred
insinuated
intimated
offered
proposed
recommended

tattled
blabbed
blurted
gossiped
leaked
rumored
snitched
spilled
squeaked

teased
bugged
harassed
mocked
needled
pestered
razzed
ribbed
roasted
taunted

warned
admonished
advised
alerted
cautioned
exhorted
forewarned

whispered
breathed
buzzed
hissed
mumbled
murmured
muttered

-ly Adverbs

angrily
bitterly
coldly
furiously
indignantly
sharply

apparently
allegedly
evidently
incidentally
seemingly

beautifully
alluringly
charmingly
daintily
delicately
elegantly
enchantingly
exquisitely
glamorously
gracefully
majestically
radiantly
stunningly

bravely
adventurously
audaciously
boldly
courageously
daringly
fearlessly
gallantly
heroically
valiantly

calmly
harmoniously
peacefully
placidly
serenely
soothingly
tranquilly

carefully
attentively
cautiously
conscientiously
gingerly
mindfully
prudently
vigilantly
warily
watchfully

casually
aimlessly
informally
nonchalantly
offhandedly
unceremoniously

certainly
clearly
naturally
obviously
surely
undeniably
undoubtedly
unmistakably
unquestionably

clumsily
absentmindedly
accidentally
awkwardly
carelessly
ungracefully

continually
ceaselessly
constantly
continuously
endlessly
eternally
incessantly
perpetually
persistently
relentlessly

creatively
artistically
cleverly
imaginatively

cruelly
brutally
malevolently
maliciously
ruthlessly
savagely
viciously
wickedly

dramatically
charismatically
emotionally
melodramatically
suspensefully
theatrically

easily
coolly
effortlessly
freely
simply
skillfully
smoothly

enthusiastically
ardently
eagerly
energetically
excitedly
passionately
zealously

fearfully
alarmedly
apprehensively
cowardly
frantically
tremblingly

finally
conclusively
decisively
eventually
lastly
ultimately

gently
delicately
faintly
meekly
mildly
softly
sweetly
tenderly

happily
cheerfully
contentedly
ecstatically
joyfully
merrily

hesitantly
dubiously
falteringly
haltingly
indecisively
irresolutely
reluctantly
skeptically
tentatively
uncertainly

honestly
admittedly
frankly
genuinely
sincerely
truly
truthfully
veraciously

humorously
amusingly
comically
jokingly
playfully

initially
firstly
originally
primarily

–ly Adverbs

intelligently
brilliantly
cleverly
ingeniously

kindly
affectionately
compassionately
fondly
graciously
lovingly
sweetly

loudly
boisterously
clamorously
deafeningly
noisily
piercingly
riotously
shrilly
thunderously
uproariously

luckily
auspiciously
favorably
fortunately
happily
opportunely
prosperously

nervously
anxiously
apprehensively
restlessly
shakily
skittishly
worriedly

occasionally
irregularly
periodically
sporadically

politely
affably
cordially
courteously
graciously
respectfully
tactfully

powerfully
forcefully
intensely
mightily
strongly
vigorously
violently

pridefully
arrogantly
boastfully
egotistically
haughtily
pompously
smugly

purposely
consciously
deliberately
intentionally
knowingly
voluntarily
willfully

quickly
briskly
busily
hastily
hurriedly
impatiently
speedily
swiftly

quietly
breathlessly
gently
inconspicuously
noiselessly
silently

regularly
commonly
faithfully
frequently
generally
habitually
invariably
normally
ordinarily
periodically
repeatedly
steadily
systematically
tirelessly
typically
unchangingly
usually

rudely
churlishly
disrespectfully
harshly
impertinently
impolitely
impudently
inconsiderately
insolently

sadly
cheerlessly
dejectedly
despondently
dismally
dolefully
mournfully
sorrowfully

tragically
unfortunately
unhappily
wistfully

shyly
bashfully
humbly
modestly
sheepishly
skittishly
timidly

slowly
casually
eventually
gradually
hesitantly
lazily
patiently
sluggishly

sneakily
cunningly
deviously
secretly
slyly
stealthily
surreptitiously
suspiciously

strangely
magically
miraculously
mysteriously
oddly
supernaturally

stupidly
foolishly
indolently
mindlessly
moronically
obnoxiously

suddenly
abruptly
immediately
instantly
startlingly
unexpectedly

surprisingly
actually
amazingly
astonishingly
incredibly
interestingly
ironically
remarkably
shockingly
unbelievably
unknowingly
unpredictably

tiredly
exhaustedly
drowsily
sleepily
weakly
wearily

wildly
ferociously
fiercely
passionately
recklessly
roughly
viciously

wisely
discerningly
judiciously
perceptively
prudently
sagaciously

Colors and Shapes

Z-Z-Z-Z-Z *Boring:* The <u>blue</u> sky had some <u>white</u> clouds.
Interesting: In the <u>azure</u> sky dangled <u>marshmallow white</u> clouds.

Black

ebony	crow	jet	onyx	shadowy
charcoal	dingy	licorice	pitch	slate
clouded	dusky	murky	raven	soot
coal	ink	obsidian	sable	starless

Blue

aqua	blueberry	electric	porcelain	steel
aquamarine	cerulean	indigo	robin's egg	teal
azure	cobalt	navy	royal	turquoise
baby blue	delft	midnight	sapphire	ultramarine
beryl	denim	peacock	sky	violet

Brown

almond	chestnut	hazel	nutmeg	sorrel
amber	chocolate	henna	oak	tan
auburn	cinnamon	khaki	ochre	tawny
beige	cocoa	mahogany	pine	teak
brick	coffee	mud	russet	terra-cotta
bronze	copper	muddy	rust	toast
buff	fawn	mulch	sandy	umber
burnt sienna	ginger	nut	sepia	walnut

Gray

ashen	drab	iron	oyster	slate
clouded	dun	lead	pearly	smoky
dapple	dusky	leaden	peppery	somber
dingy	grizzled	metallic	shaded	steel
dove	heather	mousy	silvery	stone

Green

apple	emerald	kelly	moss	sage
aquamarine	evergreen	leafy	olive	sea
avocado	fir	lime	pea	spinach
beryl	forest	lush	peacock	verdure
celery	grassy	malachite	pine	viridian
chartreuse	jade	mint	pistachio	willow

Colors and Shapes

Orange

apricot	copper	gold	pumpkin	tangerine
brass	coral	ochre	salmon	terra-cotta
bronze	flame	peach	sandy	titian
burnt sienna	glowing	persimmon	shrimp	topaz

Purple

amethyst	heliotrope	maroon	pansy	royal
bluish red	lavender	mauve	plum	violaceous
fuchsia	lilac	mulberry	pomegranate	violet
grape	magenta	orchid	puce	wine

Red

blood	cherry	flushed	pink	russet
bloodshot	claret	fuchsia	raspberry	rust
blush	coral	garnet	rose	salmon
brick	cranberry	geranium	rosy	scarlet
burgundy	crimson	magenta	rouge	strawberry
candy-apple	fiery	maroon	ruby	tomato
cardinal	flame	persimmon	ruddy	wine

White

alabaster	chalky	immaculate	oyster	powdery
ashen	cream	ivory	pale	pure
blanched	fair	light	pallid	silvery
bleached	frosted	marble	pasty	snowy
blond	frosty	marshmallow	pearl	spotless
bloodless	ghostly	milky	platinum	stainless

Yellow

amber	buff	chartreuse	lemon	straw
apricot	butter	chrome	mustard	sunny
aureate	buttercup	citron	ochre	tan
beige	butterscotch	cream	orange	tangerine
bleached	canary	gold	saffron	tawny
blond	champagne	golden	sand	topaz

Shapes

angular	conical	hexagonal	proportional	spherical
circular	cylindrical	octagonal	rectangular	spiraled
concave	elliptical	oval	squared	triangular

Sight

Z-Z-Z-Z-Z *Boring:* The cave was <u>dark</u>.
Interesting: A <u>shadowy gloom</u> settled in the <u>pitch-black</u> cave.

To See

admire	gaze	mark	peer	spot
examine	glance	note	perceive	spy
eye	glare	notice	recognize	stare
eyeball	glimpse	observe	review	survey
focus	glower	ogle	scan	view
gape	goggle	peek	search	watch
gawk	inspect	peep	sight	witness

A Sight

appearance	hallucination	impression	reflection	view
display	illusion	mirage	scene	vision
exhibition	image	picture	spectacle	vista

Clear

apparent	crystalline	lucid	transparent	unobscured
cloudless	distinct	translucent	unclouded	visible

Light

alight	illuminated	lit	moonlit	sunny
fluorescent	incandescent	lucent	phosphorescent	sunshiny
golden	lighted	luminous	starry	well-lit

Dark

black	inky	nebulous	pitch-dark	sooty
blackish	lightless	obscure	pitchy	sunless
blackness	muddy	pitch-black	somber	unlit

Sight

Bright

ablaze	beaming	brilliant	glaring	radiant
aglow	blazing	flaming	glowing	vivid

Dim

bleary	dusky	fuzzy	murky	shadowy
blurred	faded	gloomy	opaque	shady
cloudy	faint	gray	overcast	tarnished
dreary	foggy	lackluster	pale	unclear

Shiny

burnished	glassy	glistening	polished	shining
crystal	gleaming	glittering	satiny	silvery
dazzling	glimmering	glossy	sheeny	sparkling
flickering	glinting	jeweled	shimmering	twinkling

Dull

ashen	drab	hazy	mousy	opaque
cloudy	dreary	indistinct	muddy	plain
colorless	dusky	lackluster	murky	subdued
dead	faded	low	muted	toned-down
dismal	flat	matte	obscure	unlit

Sound

Z-Z-Z-Z-Z *Boring:* Suddenly, a <u>sound</u> came from the basement.
Interesting: Suddenly, an <u>ear-piercing shriek</u> came from the basement.

To Hear

catch	detect	eavesdrop	listen	overhear

A Sound

din	noise	note	resonance	tone

Pleasant

harmonic	mellifluous	melodious	sonorous	symphonious
harmonious	melodic	rhythmical	symphonic	tuneful

Unpleasant

boisterous	ear-piercing	grating	piercing	rowdy
clamorous	ear-popping	monotonous	raucous	shrill
deafening	ear-splitting	noisy	riotous	whiny

Loud

bang	clamor	crackle	scream	stomp
bawl	clang	crash	screech	thud
bellow	clank	holler	shriek	thump
blare	clap	pop	slam	whack
blast	clash	racket	slurp	wham
boom	clatter	rattle	smash	whir
burst	crack	rumble	snore	whoop

Angry

bark	grumble	jeer	shout	snort
bellow	hiss	roar	snap	sputter
growl	holler	scream	snarl	yell

Scared

cry	scream	shriek	stammer	whimper
gasp	screech	squall	stutter	yelp

Sound

Sad

bawl	groan	sigh	sob	weep
blubber	howl	sniffle	squall	whimper
cry	moan	snivel	wail	yowl

Happy

cackle	giggle	laugh	snicker	tee-hee
chortle	guffaw	roar	snigger	titter
chuckle	howl	shriek	squeal	whoop

Quiet

bubble	creak	hum	pitter-patter	swish
buzz	drone	hush	plink	tick
calm	fizz	mumble	rustle	tinkle
click	gurgle	murmur	sigh	twitter
clink	hiss	mutter	sizzle	whisper

Silent

breathless	inaudible	muted	quiet	speechless
hushed	mouthed	noiseless	soundless	still

Musical

bang	clang	peal	strum	trill
beat	clink	plunk	thump	twang
boom	hum	rattle	tinkle	warble
chant	jingle	ring	toll	whistle
chime	jangle	rumble	toot	yodel

Animal

bark	cluck	honk	purr	squeal
bleat	coo	hoot	quack	twitter
bray	croak	howl	roar	whimper
buzz	crow	meow	screech	whinny
cackle	gobble	mew	snarl	yap
caw	growl	moo	snort	yelp
cheep	grunt	neigh	squawk	yip
chirp	hiss	peep	squeak	yowl

Smell

Z-Z-Z-Z-Z *Boring:* The milk <u>smelled bad</u>.

Interesting: The <u>stench</u> of the <u>curdled</u> milk turned his stomach.

To Smell

inhale	scent	sniff	snuff	whiff

A Smell

aroma	fragrance	odor	perfume	scent

No Smell

deodorized	odorless	scentless	unseasoned	unscented

Good Smelling

appealing	enticing	luscious	rich	tempting
delightful	exquisite	mouthwatering	savory	well-seasoned
divine	heavenly	pleasing	tantalizing	zestful

Fresh

antiseptic	earthy	minty	pure	starchy
clean	fragrant	new	sanitary	sterile
crisp	laundered	piney	soapy	washed

Sweet

aromatic	citrus	fragrant	perfumed	sweet-scented
buttery	cloying	fruity	rich	sweet-smelling
candied	coconut	honeyed	saccharine	toothsome
chocolaty	flowery	nectarous	sugary	vanilla

Smell

Bad Smelling

detestable	loathsome	odious	raunchy	sickening
disgusting	malodorous	offensive	reeking	stinky
fishy	nasty	putrid	repellent	tainted
foul	nauseating	rancid	repugnant	unappealing
gross	noxious	rank	repulsive	unpleasant

Burnt

burning	fumy	gaseous	smoky	sooty

Rotten

curdled	fetid	musty	polluted	repulsive
damp	foul	noisome	putrefied	rotted
dank	gross	noxious	putrid	ruined
decayed	mildewed	offensive	rancid	spoiled
decomposed	moldy	overripe	rank	tainted

Sharp

acrid	biting	harsh	piercing	salty
astringent	cutting	intense	pungent	vinegary

Sour

acidic	fermented	soured	tart	unwholesome
curdled	rancid	sourish	turned	vinegary

Spicy

cinnamic	gingery	piquant	spiced	zesty
distinctive	peppery	seasoned	spirited	zippy

Taste

Z-Z-Z-Z-z *Boring:* The cake <u>tasted good</u>.
Interesting: He <u>savored</u> each <u>heavenly</u> mouthful of the <u>rich, chocolaty</u> cake.

To Taste

lick	sample	savor	sip	slurp

A Taste

bite	morsel	mouthful	nibble	sample

Tasteless

bland	flat	insipid	unflavored	unseasoned
dull	flavorless	tasteless	unsavory	vapid

Good-tasting

appetizing	divine	mouthwatering	rich	tasty
delectable	flavorful	palatable	savory	well-prepared
delicious	flavorsome	pleasant	scrumptious	well-seasoned
delish	luscious	pleasing	tantalizing	zestful

Bad-tasting

bland	flat	offensive	repulsive	undesirable
burnt	flavorless	oily	savorless	unpalatable
detestable	gross	rancid	sickening	unpleasant
disgusting	insipid	rank	tainted	unripe
distasteful	loathsome	raunchy	tasteless	unsavory
dull	nasty	repellent	unappealing	unseasoned
fishy	nauseating	repugnant	unappetizing	vapid

Taste

Sweet

buttery	cinnamic	fruity	saccharine	sweetened
candied	citrus	honeyed	sugar-coated	syrupy
candy-coated	cloying	nectarous	sugared	toothsome
chocolaty	coconut	rich	sugary	vanilla

Sour

acidic	briny	fermented	soured	tart
biting	curdled	rancid	sourish	vinegary

Rotten

curdled	foul	offensive	rancid	rotted
decomposed	gross	overripe	rank	spoiled
fetid	moldy	putrid	repulsive	tainted

Sharp

acidic	biting	garlicky	metallic	tangy
acrid	bitter	harsh	pungent	tart
astringent	burning	medicinal	stinging	vinegary

Spicy

biting	fiery	peppery	seasoned	spirited
cinnamic	gingery	piquant	snappy	zesty
distinctive	hot	racy	spiced	zippy

Salty

acrid	brackish	highly flavored	pungent	well-flavored
alkaline	briny	over-salted	salted	well-seasoned

Touch

To Touch

brush	frisk	hug	poke	sting
caress	grab	itch	rub	strike
cuddle	grasp	nudge	scratch	stroke
dab	graze	pat	smooth	tag
embrace	handle	paw	snuggle	tap
feel	hit	pinch	squeeze	tickle

Hot

baking	feverish	lukewarm	searing	sweltering
blazing	fiery	ovenlike	sizzling	tepid
blistering	flaming	roasting	steamy	tropical
boiling	flushed	scalding	summery	torrid
burning	humid	scorching	sweaty	warm

Cold

arctic	chilly	frigid	numbing	snowy
biting	cool	frosty	piercing	stinging
bitter	crisp	frozen	polar	tingling
bleak	cutting	glacial	shivering	trembling
brisk	freezing	icy	shuddering	wintry

Dry

arid	bare	droughty	powdery	stale
baked	barren	dusty	sapped	thirsty
bald	dehydrated	parched	shriveled	torrid

Wet

damp	drizzling	muggy	slushy	soggy
dank	foggy	pouring	snowy	sopping
dewy	humid	rainy	soaked	steamy
drenched	misty	showery	soaking	teary
dripping	moist	slippery	sodden	watery

Sticky

clammy	gluey	gummy	pasty	syrupy
gloppy	gooey	gunky	sweaty	tacky

Touch

Smooth

creamy	fluid	glossy	silky	slippery
flat	flush	polished	sleek	velvety
flowing	glassy	satiny	slick	waxy

Rough

bearded	choppy	jagged	ragged	scratchy
brambly	coarse	knotty	ridged	stony
bristly	craggy	leathery	rocky	tangled
bumpy	grainy	lumpy	rugged	unshaven
bushy	gritty	matted	sandy	wiry
chapped	hairy	prickly	scraggy	woolly

Sharp

barbed	knife-edged	pronged	ridged	spiny
briery	needlelike	ragged	serrated	splintery
horned	peaked	raggedy	spiked	tapered
jagged	pointy	razor-sharp	spiky	thorny

Hard

callous	iron	packed	solid	thick
dense	leathery	rigid	stiff	tough
firm	metal	rocky	stony	wooden

Soft

comfy	doughy	foamy	powdery	squashy
cozy	downy	furry	satiny	squishy
creamy	feathery	fuzzy	silky	tender
cushy	fluffy	mushy	spongy	velvety

Heavy

beefy	fleshy	loaded	pulpy	thick
bulky	hefty	massive	stout	weighted
chunky	leaden	meaty	swollen	weighty

Light

airy	dainty	ethereal	fluffy	powdery
bubbly	downy	feathery	frothy	sheer

Conditions

Z-Z-Z-Z-Z *Boring:* The room was a <u>mess</u>.

Interesting: The <u>disheveled</u> room was <u>littered</u> with <u>beat-up</u> toys and <u>filthy</u> clothes.

Messy

bedraggled	disorderly	grubby	raunchy	sloppy
botchy	disorganized	ill-kempt	ruffled	slovenly
careless	filthy	lax	rumpled	uncombed
cluttered	foul	littered	shabby	unkempt
dirty	frowzy	muddled	slack	untidy
disheveled	frumpy	mussy	slapdash	wrinkled
disordered	grimy	nasty	slipshod	wrinkly

Neat

chipper	groomed	orderly	snug	trim
clean-cut	immaculate	organized	spick-and-span	uncluttered
combed	kempt	prim	spruce	unwrinkled
detailed	meticulous	shipshape	tidy	well-groomed
fastidious	natty	snappy	trig	well-pressed

Old

abandoned	dated	historical	primordial	tattered
aged	decayed	moth-eaten	raggedy	threadbare
ancient	decrepit	neglected	rickety	time-worn
antiquated	deteriorated	old-fashioned	run-down	traditional
antique	dilapidated	outdated	rusty	used
archaic	discarded	outmoded	scruffy	worm-eaten
broken-down	dowdy	out-of-date	shabby	worn
cast-off	faded	outworn	shoddy	worn-out
crusty	hackneyed	primitive	stale	wrinkly

New

advanced	fresh	newfound	stylish	untouched
brand-new	latest	new-sprung	trendy	untrodden
contemporary	modern	novel	ultramodern	unused
current	modernistic	original	unfamiliar	up-to-date
cutting edge	new-fashioned	recent	unspoiled	youthful

Conditions

Dirty

black	greasy	mucky	smeared	stained
contaminated	grimy	muddy	smudged	sullied
cruddy	grubby	murky	soiled	sully
dingy	grungy	nasty	soily	tainted
draggled	icky	polluted	sooty	tarnished
dreggy	impure	raunchy	sordid	unclean
dungy	mangy	scummy	splotched	unsanitary
dusty	mildewed	scuzzy	spotted	unsightly
filthy	moldy	slimy	squalid	unswept

Clean

blank	fresh	sanitary	squeaky	unsoiled
bright	hygienic	shining	stainless	unsullied
cleansed	immaculate	shiny	taintless	untainted
clear	impeccable	sparkling	tidy	untarnished
dirtless	laundered	spick-and-span	unblemished	washed
flawless	pure	spotless	unpolluted	white

Damaged

beat-up	cracked	dismembered	mutilated	shivered
bent	crippled	flawed	peeling	shot
blemished	crumbled	fractured	pulverized	shredded
broken	demolished	fragmented	ripped	slivered
burnt	destroyed	impaired	ruptured	smashed
burst	dinged	injured	separated	split
busted	discolored	mangled	severed	tattered
collapsed	disintegrated	marred	shattered	wrecked

Undamaged

complete	mint	secure	steady	unimpaired
entire	perfect	set	unblemished	uninjured
faultless	permanent	settled	unbroken	unmarked
firm	plenary	shipshape	uncut	unmarred
fixed	preserved	solid	undefiled	unruffled
flawless	replete	sound	undivided	unscathed
full	rooted	stable	unharmed	untouched
intact	safe	steadfast	unified	whole

Body

Z-Z-Z-Z-z *Boring:* The ballerina was <u>thin</u>.
Interesting: <u>Petite</u> and <u>slender</u>, the ballerina twirled like a <u>dainty</u> flower.

Thin

angular	frail	malnourished	scrawny	slight
bony	gangly	narrow	skeletal	slim
emaciated	gaunt	petite	skin-and-bone	stick
dainty	lanky	puny	skinny	twiggy
ethereal	lean	rawboned	slender	underweight

Heavy

beefy	burly	heavy-set	plump	round
big-boned	chubby	husky	plumpish	shapeless
bloated	chunky	lumpy	portly	solid
brawny	dense	massive	potbellied	stocky
broad	elephantine	obese	pudgy	stout
bulging	full-bodied	oversized	robust	thick
bulky	gargantuan	paunchy	rotund	wide

Short

compact	little	pint-sized	stunted	tiny
dwarfed	low	runty	stubby	undersized
dwarfish	miniature	squat	stumpy	wee

Tall

alpine	gangly	lanky	skyscraping	stretched
beanstalk	giant	lofty	stick	towering

Weak

decrepit	effeminate	feeble	fragile	puny
delicate	emaciated	flaccid	frail	sickly

Strong

beefy	burly	muscular	robust	solid
brawny	firm	powerful	rugged	strapping

Fit

athletic	healthy	shapely	toned	trim

Hair

Z-Z-Z-Z-z *Boring:* She had <u>pretty hair</u>.

Interesting: <u>Long, flowing locks of strawberry blonde hair curled</u> down her back.

Hair

cut	locks	mop	tendrils	tufts
fuzz	mane	strands	tresses	wisps

Condition

bouncy	flaky	groomed	shiny	stringy
clean	flowing	messy	silky	tangled
coarse	fluffy	neat	sleek	thick
dingy	flyaway	oily	smooth	thin
drab	frizzy	puffy	soft	tidy
dry	glistening	raggedy	springy	trimmed
dull	glossy	ratty	straggly	wiry
fine	grimy	shaggy	straw-like	unkempt

Length

buzzed	cropped	mid-length	shaved	shoulder-length
chin-length	long	receding	short	waist-length

Style

afro	cowlick	kinky	pinned	stiff
bangs	crimped	knotted	pleated	straight
bobbed	curled	layered	ponytail	teased
bowl cut	curly	nappy	ringlets	tussled
braided	feathered	mohawk	shaved	twisted
bun	flattop	permed	slicked	uneven
buzz	gelled	pigtail	spiked	wavy

Color

amber	chestnut	flaxen	platinum	straw
ash-blonde	coal black	frosted	raven	strawberry blonde
auburn	copper	golden	red	streaked
black	dark	gray	russet	tawny
bleached	dirty blonde	highlighted	sandy blonde	towheaded
blond	fair	jet black	silver	washed out
bronze	fake	light	silvery	white
brunette	fiery red	pale	snowy white	yellow

Face

Z·Z·Z·Z·z *Boring:* He had an <u>unusual face</u>.
Interesting: He had <u>droopy eyes</u>, <u>pointy ears</u>, and a <u>crooked nose</u>.

Cheeks

bony	chubby	full	hollow	round
chipmunk	dimpled	high	puffy	sunken

Chin

dimpled	double	long	pointy	square

Ears

elephant	elf	floppy	pointy	shell-like

Eyebrows

arched	bushy	high	penciled-in	thin
broad	defined	narrow	thick	wide

Eyelashes

dark	full	long	short	thick

Eyes

almond-shaped	bright	droopy	puffy	slit
beady	bug	narrow	round	squinty
bloodshot	cat	oval	slanted	wide

Facial Hair

beard	clean-shaven	mustache	scruffy	sideburns
bristles	goatee	scratchy	shaven	whiskers

Forehead

broad	flat	high	long	pronounced

Face

Lips

cracked	full	pouty	pursed	thin	
fat	plump	puckered	supple	wide	

Mouth

crooked	gaping	open	slack-jawed	wide

Nose

blunt	button	flat	pug	straight
broad	crinkled	hooked	Roman	tiny
bulbous	crooked	long	ski jump	upturned
bumpy	delicate	pointy	slender	wide

Nostrils

broad	flared	narrow	pointy	wide

Skin

aged	clear	healthy	pimply	splotchy
albino	cold	leathery	pockmarked	supple
ashen	dark	light	rosy	swarthy
ashy	dimpled	milky white	rough	tan
baby	fair	moley	ruddy	taut
blanched	flushed	oily	sallow	washed-out
bleached	freckled	old	scarred	weathered
blotchy	freckly	olive	sensitive	white
blushing	ghastly white	pale	sickly	wrinkled
bruised	ghostly white	pallid	smooth	wrinkly
clammy	glowing	pasty white	soft	youthful

Teeth

bucked	chipped	crooked	pointy	straight

Character Traits

bossy
aggressive
controlling
demanding
domineering
forceful
intimidating
overbearing
tyrannical

brave
adventurous
audacious
bold
chivalrous
courageous
daring
dauntless
fearless
gallant
heroic
knightly
valiant
valorous

cowardly
fearful
gutless
passive
spineless
timid
weak

crazy
demented
disturbed
insane
lunatic
maniacal

creative
artistic
clever
gifted
imaginative

ingenious
innovative
inspired
inventive
original
unique

determined
driven
persevering
persistent
steadfast

dishonest
corrupt
deceitful
deceptive
devious
disingenuous
untruthful

disobedient
defiant
insubordinate
lawless
rebellious
undisciplined
unmanageable
unruly

driven
industrious
sedulous
studious

energetic
active
animated
enthusiastic
high-spirited
lively
sprightly
vivacious

enthusiastic
ardent
eager
earnest
excited
exuberant
passionate
zealous

evil
corrupt
fiendish
hateful
immoral
monstrous
sinful
sinister
vile
wicked

forgiving
gracious
magnanimous
merciful

friendly
affable
amiable
amicable
congenial
convivial
cordial
genial
good-natured
warm

fun
amusing
convivial
enjoyable
entertaining
exciting
imaginative
lively
playful

funny
amusing
comical
entertaining
hilarious
humorous
hysterical
witty

generous
benevolent
charitable
magnanimous
noble
selfless
self-sacrificing
unselfish

hard-working
ambitious
assiduous
diligent

honest
honorable
forthright
sincere
straightforward
trustworthy
truthful

hostile
aggressive
antagonistic
argumentative
belligerent
combative
contentious
pugnacious
quarrelsome

humble
meek
modest
self-effacing

irresponsible
careless
flighty
forgetful
inattentive
undependable
unreliable
untrustworthy

jealous
covetous
envious
green-eyed
possessive

kind
caring
compassionate
considerate
courteous
gentle
gracious
loving
soft-hearted
sweet
sympathetic
tender
thoughtful
warm

lazy
heavy-footed
idle
indolent
languorous
slothful
slow-moving
unmotivated

loyal
committed
dedicated
devoted
faithful
steadfast

Character Traits

mean
barbarous
brutal
cold-hearted
cruel
heartless
insensitive
malevolent
malicious
ruthless
uncaring
unkind
vicious

moral
chaste
ethical
noble
principled
pure
righteous
virtuous

negative
critical
cynical
defeated
hopeless
pessimistic
sarcastic

outgoing
convivial
extroverted
gregarious
personable
sociable
social
unreserved

polite
affable
civil
cordial
courteous
gracious
respectful

positive
cheerful
hopeful
idealistic
optimistic
sanguine

practical
level-headed
logical
pragmatic
rational
realistic
reasonable
sensible

prideful
arrogant
boastful
conceited
egotistical
haughty
narcissistic
pompous
smug
vain

respectable
admirable
honorable
laudable
praiseworthy
reputable
upright

responsible
conscientious
dependable
dutiful
mature
reliable
trustworthy

revengeful
malicious
punitive
retaliatory
spiteful
vengeful
vindictive

rude
boorish
churlish
discourteous
disrespectful
impertinent
impolite
impudent
inconsiderate
insolent
surly
uncivil

selfish
egocentric
greedy
miserly
parsimonious
self-centered
stingy

serious
austere
humorless
intense
solemn
somber
stern

silly
childish
clownish
immature
nonsensical
senseless

smart
bookish
bright
brilliant
clever
ingenious
intellectual
intelligent
knowledgeable
quick-witted
sharp

strange
awkward
bizarre
eccentric
mysterious
odd
outlandish
peculiar
unusual
weird

stubborn
hardheaded
headstrong
obstinate
persistent
stiff-necked
strong-willed
willful

stupid
brainless
foolish
idiotic
imbecilic
mindless
moronic
simple
unintelligent
witless

talented
accomplished
adept
artistic
brilliant
experienced
expert
gifted
ingenious
skilled
skillful

tricky
conniving
crafty
cunning
devious

mischievous
scheming
shrewd
sly
sneaky
wily

uncaring
apathetic
callous
cold
heartless
indifferent
insensitive
unsympathetic

understanding
accepting
empathetic
perceptive
sensitive
sympathetic

unforgiving
begrudging
bitter
embittered
merciless
resentful

unsocial
introverted
reclusive
reserved
solitary
standoffish
unsociable
withdrawn

wise
discerning
enlightened
insightful
judicious
perceptive
prudent
sagacious

Emotions / Feelings

Z-Z-Z-Z-z **Boring:** The singer on the stage was <u>scared</u>.
Interesting: <u>Trembling in terror</u>, the <u>panic-stricken</u> singer stood <u>frozen</u> on stage.

afraid
aghast
alarmed
apprehensive
blanched
cowardly
cowed
daunted
disheartened
dismayed
distressed
faint-hearted
fearful
frightened
frozen
horrified
intimidated
panicked
panicky
panic-stricken
petrified
rattled
scared
shaken
shocked
spooked
startled
stunned
terrified
terror-stricken
trembling

angry
boiling
cross
enraged
fiery
fuming
furious
heated
incensed
indignant
inflamed
infuriated
irate
maddened
outraged
provoked
rabid
raging
riled
vexed
wrathful

annoyed
agitated
bothered
crabby
cranky
disgruntled
displeased
dissatisfied
frustrated
grouchy
grumpy

ill-tempered
irritable
irritated
moody
peeved
peevish
petulant
sulky
sullen
temperamental
vexed

ashamed
apologetic
contrite
disappointed
mournful
penitent
regretful
remorseful
repentant
rueful
sorrowful
sorry

calm
harmonious
mellow
peaceful
placid
quiescent
quiet
relaxed

reposeful
restful
serene
soothing
still
stormless
tranquil
undisturbed
unruffled
waveless
windless

confused
abashed
addled
baffled
befuddled
bewildered
confounded
dazed
disconcerted
disoriented
distracted
dizzy
flummoxed
flustered
muddled
mystified
perplexed
puzzled
stumped
unglued

disappointed
disconcerted
discontented
discouraged
disenchanted
disgruntled
disheartened
disillusioned
dissatisfied
downhearted
embittered
frustrated
resentful
saddened
thwarted
ungratified
unsatisfied
vanquished

embarrassed
abashed
ashamed
chagrined
disconcerted
disgraced
humbled
humiliated
mortified
shamed

excited
agitated
animated

Emotions / Feelings

aroused
awakened
charged
delighted
eager
emotional
enthusiastic
feverish
hyper
hysterical
jumpy
lively
passionate
stirred
thrilled
wild

happy
blessed
blissful
blithe
cheerful
cheery
chipper
chirpy
content
contented
convivial
delighted
ecstatic
elated
exultant
gleeful
gratified
jolly
joyful

joyous
jubilant
lighthearted
merry
mirthful
overjoyed
peppy
perky
playful
pleasant
pleased
sunny
thrilled
upbeat

lonely
disconsolate
forlorn
forsaken
isolated
lonesome
reclusive
rejected
secluded
solitary
unsocial
withdrawn

nervous
anxious
apprehensive
concerned
distressed
flustered
high-strung
jittery

jumpy
nervy
restless
skittish
tense
uneasy
uptight
worried

proud
contented
dignified
gratified
honored
pleased
satisfied

sad
bereaved
brokenhearted
crestfallen
crushed
dejected
depressed
despairing
despondent
devastated
disconsolate
dismal
doleful
downcast
forlorn
gloomy
glum
grief-stricken
grieved

heartbroken
heartsick
heartsore
heavy-hearted
inconsolable
languishing
low-spirited
lugubrious
melancholy
miserable
morose
mournful
somber
sorrowful
troubled
weeping
wistful

shy
bashful
cautious
coy
demure
humble
introverted
meek
modest
mousy
quiet
rabbity
reserved
reticent
self-conscious
sheepish
skittish
timid
unassertive

surprised
agape
aghast
amazed
astonished
astounded
awestruck
dumbfounded
dumbstruck
flabbergasted
floored
overwhelmed
shocked
speechless
staggered
startled
stunned
thrown
thunderstruck

upset
agitated
bothered
disconcerted
dismayed
disquieted
distraught
distressed
disturbed
stressed
troubled
unglued
unsettled
worried

Big / Small

Big		Small	
ample	major	baby	piddling
behemoth	mammoth	bite-sized	pint-sized
broad	massive	bitty	pocket-sized
bulky	mighty	cramped	puny
burly	mountainous	diminutive	runty
capacious	monstrous	dwarfish	scanty
colossal	monumental	inconsequential	scrubby
considerable	overgrown	inconsiderable	short
enormous	oversized	insignificant	shrimp
expansive	prodigious	light	skimpy
extensive	roomy	limited	slight
giant	sizable	little	smallish
gigantic	spacious	meager	stubby
grand	staggering	microscopic	stunted
great	stupendous	mini	teeny
hefty	substantial	miniature	teensy
huge	titanic	miniscule	tiny
hulking	towering	minor	toy
humongous	tremendous	minute	trifling
husky	unrestricted	modest	trivial
immeasurable	vast	narrow	truncated
immense	voluminous	paltry	undersized
jumbo	whopping	petite	wee
magnificent			

Beautiful / Ugly

Z-Z-Z-Z-z **Boring:** The haircut was <u>ugly</u>.
Interesting: The <u>frightful</u> haircut bordered on <u>grotesque</u>.

Beautiful		Ugly	
adorable	grand	abnormal	monstrous
alluring	handsome	appalling	nasty
appealing	ideal	awful	nauseating
attractive	impressive	bad-looking	obnoxious
beckoning	interesting	beastly	odd
becoming	inviting	bizarre	outlandish
bewitching	lovely	creepy	piggish
breathtaking	luring	deformed	plain
captivating	magnificent	disagreeable	repellent
charming	majestic	disfigured	repugnant
classy	marvelous	disgusting	repulsive
comely	mesmeric	distasteful	revolting
cute	pleasant	distorted	shocking
dazzling	pleasing	eerie	sickening
delightful	pretty	foul	sordid
divine	radiant	freakish	sorry
elegant	ravishing	frightful	strange
enchanting	refined	grisly	terrible
engaging	resplendent	gross	unalluring
enthralling	shapely	grotesque	unappealing
enticing	sightly	grungy	unattractive
excellent	splendid	hag-like	uncomely
exquisite	statuesque	hard-featured	undesirable
fair	stunning	hideous	uninviting
fascinating	sublime	homely	unnatural
fetching	superb	horrid	unpleasant
fine	tantalizing	horrifying	unseemly
glamorous	well-formed	ill-favored	unsightly
good-looking	well-groomed	inelegant	vile
gorgeous	winsome	loathsome	weird
graceful	wonderful	misshapen	wretched

Good / Bad

Z-Z-Z-Z-Z **Boring:** The weather was <u>bad</u>, but we had a <u>good</u> day.
Interesting: Despite the <u>foul</u> weather, we still had a <u>sensational</u> day at the park.

Good		Bad	
admirable	mind-blowing	abominable	horrifying
amazing	miraculous	appalling	loathsome
astonishing	notable	atrocious	lousy
astounding	noteworthy	awful	lurid
awe-inspiring	outrageous	base	mean
awesome	outstanding	beastly	nasty
beautiful	overwhelming	contemptible	nauseating
breathtaking	phenomenal	cursed	obnoxious
brilliant	prodigious	deplorable	obscene
commendable	remarkable	despicable	odious
distinguished	sensational	detestable	offensive
excellent	spectacular	disagreeable	raunchy
exceptional	splendid	disgusting	repellent
exciting	stirring	dreadful	reprehensible
extraordinary	striking	foul	repugnant
fabulous	stunning	frightening	repulsive
fantastic	stupendous	frightful	revolting
fine	superb	ghastly	scandalous
glorious	superior	grim	scary
illustrious	terrific	grisly	shameful
impressive	thrilling	gruesome	shocking
incredible	unbelievable	hateful	sickening
inspiring	unreal	heinous	terrible
legendary	unrivaled	hideous	terrifying
lofty	valuable	horrendous	unpleasant
magnificent	wonderful	horrible	vile
marvelous	wondrous	horrid	wretched
memorable	abhorrent	horrific	

Interesting / Boring

Z-Z-Z-Z-z *Boring:* The book was <u>boring</u>.

Interesting: The <u>dull</u>, <u>monotonous</u> book left me feeling <u>uninspired</u>.

Interesting	Boring
absorbing	colorless
alluring	commonplace
amusing	dead
appealing	drab
arresting	dreary
captivating	drudging
charismatic	dull
compelling	flat
curious	ho-hum
delightful	humdrum
enchanting	insipid
engaging	interminable
engrossing	lackluster
entertaining	lifeless
enthralling	monotone
entrancing	monotonous
exceptional	platitudinous
exciting	repetitious
exotic	routine
fascinating	spiritless
gripping	stale
impressive	stereotypical
intriguing	stodgy
provocative	tedious
refreshing	tiresome
riveting	trite
spellbinding	unanimated
stimulating	unexciting
stirring	uninspired
striking	uninteresting
thought-provoking	vapid
unusual	wearisome

A Little / A Lot

Z-Z-Z-Z-z *Boring:* The night sky had <u>a lot</u> of stars.
Interesting: The stars were <u>numberless</u> in the night sky.

A Little	A Lot
a few	abundant
a handful of	bounteous
a scattering of	bountiful
a sprinkling of	copious
inconsequential	countless
inconsiderable	endless
infrequent	immeasurable
insufficient	incalculable
limited	infinite
meager	innumerable
minor	limitless
minute	many
negligible	multifarious
occasional	multiple
paltry	multitudinous
petty	myriad
piddling	numberless
rare	numerous
scant	plentiful
scanty	plenty of
scarce	scads of
scarcely any	several
skimpy	swarming with
slight	teeming with
slim	uncountable
some	unlimited
sparse	voluminous

Easy / Hard

Z-Z-Z-Z-Z *Boring:* The homework was <u>easy</u>, but the test was <u>hard</u>.
Interesting: The homework was **manageable**, but the test was **complicated**.

Easy	Hard
accessible	arduous
apparent	backbreaking
basic	bothersome
clear-cut	burdensome
direct	challenging
effortless	complex
elemental	complicated
elementary	confusing
evident	demanding
facile	difficult
manageable	exacting
obvious	exhausting
painless	formidable
plain	grueling
routine	involved
self-explanatory	laborious
simple	painful
smooth	perplexing
straightforward	problematic
uncomplicated	puzzling
undemanding	strenuous
understandable	troublesome
uninvolved	trying
workable	unclear

Compare / Contrast

Z-Z-Z-Z-z **Boring:** Tennis is played on a court, <u>and</u> baseball is played on a field.
Interesting: Tennis is played on a court, <u>whereas</u> baseball is played on a field.

Comparing Words	Contrasting Words
alike	although
at first glance	at first glance
besides	but
both	by contrast
by comparison	contrast
comparable	conversely
compare	despite
compared to	differ
in common	differences
in comparison to	different
in the same manner	different from
in the same way	even though
just as	however
like	in contrast
likewise	instead
on the one hand	on the contrary
resemble	on the other hand
resemblance	opposite
share	unlike
similarities	variations
similarity	varied
similarly	vary
similar to	whereas
the same	while
the same as	yet

Be Specific! How to avoid using the word "thing."

Z-Z-Z-Z-z *Boring:* Frogs and toads have many <u>things</u> in common.
Interesting: Frogs and toads have many <u>characteristics</u> in common.

achievement
accomplishment
advancement
contribution
feat
improvement
progress
success

belief
conviction
feeling
idea
notion
opinion
position
theory
understanding
view

chance
opportunity
possibility
prospect

characteristic
aspect
attribute
distinction
feature
peculiarity
property
quality
trademark
trait

choice
alternative
decision
option
possibility
preference
selection

effect
aftermath
consequence
outcome
ramification
result

effort
action
attempt
endeavor
step
stride
undertaking

enjoyment
activity
amusement
diversion
entertainment
hobby
interest
pastime
recreation

experience
adventure
affair
encounter
enterprise
escapade
event
exploration
exposure
involvement
ordeal
participation
undertaking
venture

goal
aim
ambition

ideal
intention
objective
plan

issue
argument
controversy
focus
question
subject
theme
topic

item
article
belonging
object
particular
possession
product

part
aspect
component
detail
element
factor
feature
particular
section
segment

place
area
locale
location
scene
setting
spot
site
vicinity

problem
challenge
concern
conflict
difficulty
dilemma
disadvantage
frustration
hardship
obstacle
predicament
quagmire
quandary
struggle
trial
trouble
weakness

proof
data
evidence
fact
statistic
testimony
verification

reason
argument
explanation
justification
motive
pretext
rationale

situation
circumstance
episode
event
happening
incident
issue
matter
occasion
occurrence

talent
ability
capability
genius
gift
power
skill
strength

type
category
description
example
form
genre
group
kind
model
pattern
sort
variety

value
advantage
benefit
importance
meaning
merit
purpose
significance
use
worth

way
approach
course
direction
manner
method
mode
style
system
technique

50 Boring Words and Phrases to Avoid

Don't get stuck in old writing habits! When you find yourself about to use these tired words and phrases, search for more specific and lively ones!